Canada

# Famous Canadians from British Columbia

Barb McDermott and Gail McKeown
Reidmore Books

Reidmore Books Inc.

18228 - 102 Avenue
Edmonton, AB  T5S 1S7
phone (780) 444-0912
toll-free 1-800-661-2859
fax (780) 444-0933

website: http://www.reidmore.com
email: reidmore@compusmart.ab.ca

printed and bound in Canada

We acknowledge the financial support of the
Government of Canada through the
Book Publishing Industry Development Program (BPIDP)
for our publishing activities.

Canada

**Canadian Cataloguing in Publication Data**
McDermott, Barb.
All about famous Canadians from British Columbia

(All about series)
Includes index.
ISBN 1-896132-64-2

1. British Columbia—Biography—Juvenile literature.  I. McKeown, Gail.
II. Title.  III. Series: McDermott, Barb. All about series.
FC3805.M23 1999 j920.0711   C99-910755-0   F1086.8.M28 1999

## About the Authors

Barb McDermott and Gail McKeown are highly experienced
kindergarten teachers living in Ontario. Both hold Bachelor of Arts and
Bachelor of Education degrees, Early Childhood diplomas, specialist
certificates in Primary Education, and have completed qualification
courses in Special Education. As well, Gail has a specialist certificate in
Reading and Visual Arts, and Barb has one in Guidance.

## Credits

Editorial: Leah-Ann Lymer, Scott Woodley, David Strand,
Debbie Culbertson
Illustration, design and layout: Bruno Enderlin, Leslieanna Blackner Au
Maps: Wendy Johnson, Johnson Cartographics

## Photo Credits

*Cover and stamp photo:* David Suzuki, courtesy of David Suzuki
**Page**
3 Art Gallery of Greater Victoria
5 BC Archives
7 Irene Uchida
9 Irene Uchida
11 Hon. Mr. Justice Wallace Oppal
13 Hon. Mr. Justice Wallace Oppal
15 The Rick Hansen Institute
17 The Rick Hansen Institute
19 J.M. Carisse Photo
21 CANAPRESS/CP
23 CANAPRESS/CP
25 David Suzuki
27 Tim Matheson/Image Network Inc.

We have made every effort to identify and credit the sources of
all photographs, illustrations, and information used in this textbook.
Reidmore Books appreciates any further information or corrections;
acknowledgment will be given in subsequent editions.

# Table of Contents

(All about what's in the book)

## Introduction
(All about the beginning)

People who make the world a better place to live can become famous.

Canada has famous artists, scientists, **justices,** athletes, and **politicians.**

Many famous Canadians are from the **province** of British Columbia.

YUKON

NORTHWEST TERRITORIES

N
W E
S

BRITISH
COLUMBIA

ARCTIC
OCEAN

YUKON

NORTHWEST
TERRITORIES

NUNAVUT

PACIFIC
OCEAN

BRITISH
COLUMBIA

ALBERTA

Hudson
Bay

NEWFOUNDLAND

ATLANTIC
OCEAN

SASKATCHEWAN

MANITOBA

ONTARIO

QUEBEC

PRINCE EDWARD
ISLAND

NOVA
SCOTIA

NEW
BRUNSWICK

PACIFIC
OCEAN

Kim Campbell,
Port Alberni

Irene Uchida,
Vancouver

ALBERTA

SASKATCHEWAN

Rick Hansen,
Port Alberni

Wallace Oppal,
Vancouver

Emily Carr,
Victoria

David Suzuki,
Vancouver

1

## Emily Carr (1871-1945)
(All about a famous Canadian artist)

Emily Carr was born in Victoria.

She was an artist and a writer.

Her paintings include 1 called Above the Gravel Pit.

She painted in a way that many people did not like.

People began to like her paintings when she was 56 years old.

Above the Gravel Pit, by Emily Carr

## Emily Carr (1871-1945)
(All about a famous Canadian artist)

Emily Carr spent many months with Northwest Coast Native people.

She acted out what she wanted to say to the Native people because she did not know how to speak their language.

She was always laughing at her acting, so the Native people called her Klee Wyck.

Klee Wyck means "Laughing One."

Emily Carr's 1st book was called Klee Wyck, and it won the Governor General's Award in 1941.

Emily Carr (lower right) and Her Sisters

## Irene Uchida (1917-)
(All about a famous Canadian scientist)

Irene Uchida was born in Vancouver.

She is a scientist.

She is an expert on why some children are born with health problems.

She wants to find out why people with **Down's syndrome** have 1 more **chromosome** than other people.

She has won many awards for her work, including the Order of Canada.

Irene Uchida

## Irene Uchida (1917-)
(All about a famous Canadian scientist)

Irene Uchida studied at the **University** of Toronto.

She wanted to learn how to help families.

One of her professors showed her that the best way she could help would be by becoming a scientist.

Irene Uchida was the 1st Canadian to know how to find out if people had a disease called 18 trisomy.

She helps Canadians to understand more about Down's syndrome and other diseases.

Irene Uchida Studied at the University of Toronto

## Wallace Oppal (1940-)
(All about a famous Canadian justice)

Wallace Oppal was born in Vancouver.

He is the 1st **Sikh**-Canadian to become a justice of the Supreme Court of British Columbia.

He helps to make Canada a better place by working with groups that help families.

He helps to educate lawyers.

Wallace Oppal

11

## Wallace Oppal (1940-)
(All about a famous Canadian justice)

Wallace Oppal studied to become a lawyer at the University of British Columbia.

He worked as a lawyer for 13 years before becoming a justice.

He enjoys playing baseball and basketball.

He tried to become a part of the Cleveland Indians baseball team when he was 18 years old.

Wallace Oppal Is a Justice

## Rick Hansen (1957-)
(All about a famous Canadian athlete)

Rick Hansen was born in Port Alberni.

He is an athlete who went around the world in a wheelchair.

He visited 34 countries and travelled 40 000 km in his wheelchair.

He went around the world to raise money for **spinal cord research.**

His trip raised $24 000 000.

Rick Hansen

## Rick Hansen (1957- )

(All about a famous Canadian athlete)

Rick Hansen became a **paraplegic** when he was 15 years old.

He is the 1st person in a wheelchair to graduate from the University of British Columbia's physical education program.

He wants wheelchair racing to become an Olympic sport.

He works to help people have better lives.

He has won many awards, including the Order of Canada.

Canad

Rick Hansen Speaking to Children in Australia

17

## Kim Campbell (1947-)
(All about a famous Canadian politician)

Kim Campbell was born in Port Alberni.

She is the 1st woman to be the **prime minister** of Canada.

She is also the 1st woman to be the minister of national defence and the minister of justice in Canada.

She was careful about spending the government's money.

Kim Campbell

## Kim Campbell (1947–)
(All about a famous Canadian politician)

Kim Campbell studied to become a lawyer at the University of British Columbia.

She also studied in Britain.

She was Canada's prime minister for 4 months in 1993.

She wrote a book about herself called Time and Chance.

Kim Campbell Was a Prime Minister

### David Suzuki (1936-)
(All about a famous Canadian scientist)

David Suzuki was born in Vancouver.

He is a scientist, writer, and television host.

His television shows include "The Nature of Things with David Suzuki" and "A Planet for the Taking."

His television shows are some of the most popular shows ever made in Canada.

He has won many awards for his work, including the Order of Canada.

David Suzuki

## David Suzuki (1936-)
(All about a famous Canadian scientist)

David Suzuki studied at universities in the United States.

He 1st wanted to become a medical doctor.

He enjoyed a **genetics** class so much that he decided to become a geneticist instead.

He uses his television shows to explain science in a way that is easy to understand.

He uses his television shows to teach people how to live without harming the Earth.

David Suzuki As a Young Boy

25

## Summary
(All about the ending)

Canada has people who try to make the world a better place to live.

Many famous Canadians are from British Columbia.

Canada has Emily Carr, Irene Uchida, Wallace Oppal, Rick Hansen, Kim Campbell, and David Suzuki.

Canada has amazing people!

British Columbia Has Amazing People

# Glossary
(All about what the words mean)

**chromosome** (page 6)
You have 1 000 000s of chromosomes in your body. Chromosomes tell what your body will look like.

**Down's syndrome** (page 6)
People with Down's syndrome have 1 more chromosome than other people. People with Down's syndrome learn differently from other people.

**genetics** (page 24)
Genetics is the science that studies how things like eye, hair, and skin colour are passed from parents to their children. Geneticists are people who are experts in studying genetics.

**justices** (page 1)
A justice is a person who tries to decide who is right and who is wrong in court cases.

**paraplegic** (page 16)
A paraplegic is someone who cannot move his or her legs.

**politicians** (page 1)
Politicians are people who have been elected to government, or who are trying to be elected.

**prime minister** (page 18)
The prime minister is the leader of Canada's government.

**province** (page 1)
A province is a separate region in Canada that has its own government.

**research** (page 14)
To research is to try to find out more about something.

**Sikh** (page 10)
A Sikh is a follower of the Sikh religion. The Sikh religion comes from an area near the northern part of India. The word Sikh means "disciple."

**spinal cord** (page 14)
The spinal cord is the part of your body that carries information between your brain and the rest of your body.

**university** (page 8)
A university is a school that students can go to after they have finished high school.